Pebble® Plus

 Helping the Environment

I Can Care for Nature

by Mary Boone

D1518741

CAPSTONE PRESS
a capstone imprint

Pebble Plus is published by Pebble
1710 Roe Crest Drive, North Mankato, Minnesota 56003
www.mycapstone.com

Library of Congress Cataloging-in-Publication Data
Library of Congress Cataloging-in-Publication Data is
available on the Library of Congress website.
ISBN 978-1-9771-0311-6 (library binding)
ISBN 978-1-9771-0521-9 (paperback)
ISBN 978-1-9771-0319-2 (eBook PDF)

Editorial Credits
Anna Butzer, editor; Kayla Rossow, designer;
Tracy Cummins, media researcher; Kathy McColley, production specialist

Image Credits
iStockphoto: FatCamera, 17, vgajic, 13; Shutterstock: Belozorova Elena, 15, Kumer Oksana, Back
Cover, LightField Studios, 7, Monkey Business Images, 11, 21, Ms Moloko, Design Element, tbmnk, 5,
TinnaPong, Cover, Unkas Photo, 9, wavebreakmedia, 19

Note to Parents and Teachers

The Helping the Environment set supports national curriculum standards for science and
community. This book describes and illustrates caring for nature. The images support early
readers in understanding the text. The repetition of words and phrases helps early readers
learn new words. This book also introduces early readers to subject-specific vocabulary
words, which are defined in the Glossary section. Early readers may need assistance to read
some words and to use the Table of Contents, Glossary, Read More, Internet Sites, Critical
Thinking Questions, and Index sections of the book.

Printed and bound in China
970

Table of Contents

Beautiful Nature

Look around! Nature surrounds us. Plants, trees, water, and animals are all part of nature. I am part of nature too.

I go on a walk with my parents. We stop and smell flowers. We listen for wildlife. I hear a hawk screeching and grasshoppers chirping.

Caring for Nature

I care for nature by picking up litter. Birds and other animals can mistake trash for food. If they eat trash, it can make them sick.

Dad and I go on a hike.
We are careful to stay
on the trails. If we wander
off, we might step on a small
animal's home or food source.

My family and I plant a tree in our yard. Trees are very important. They provide oxygen. Trees give food and shelter to wildlife.

It is hard for birds to find food in winter. I use an empty plastic bottle to make a bird feeder. Mom helps me hang the bird feeder outside.

My friends help me plant flowers. We make sure they are bee-friendly. We water the flowers. We do not use harmful chemicals on them.

Working Together

Our neighbors gather at a
nearby park. We wear gloves
and carry garbage bags.
Together we pick up all
of the trash and litter.

We plant trees and flowers. We should all spend time in nature. Caring for nature is easy when you know about nature.

Glossary

chemical—a substance used in or produced by chemistry

litter—to throw garbage on the ground

mistake—to identify something incorrectly

oxygen—a colorless gas that people and animals breathe; humans and animals need oxygen to live

shelter—a place where an animal can stay safe from weather and other animals

source—things that provide what is wanted or needed

surround—to be on every side of something

wander—to go away from a path

Read More

Pettiford, Rebecca. *Green Buildings.* Green Planet. Minneapolis, Minn.: Pogo, 2017.

Rivera, Andrea. *Plants.* Zoom In On Our Renewable Earth. Minneapolis, Minn.: Abdo Zoom, 2017.

Berne, Emma Carlson. *Earth Day.* Holidays in Rhythm and Rhyme. North Mankato, Minn.: Cantata Learning, 2018.

Internet Sites

FactHound offers a safe, fun way to find Internet sites related to this book. All of the sites on FactHound have been researched by our staff.

Here's all you do:

Visit *www.facthound.com*

Type in this code: 9781977103116

Check out projects, games and lots more at
www.capstonekids.com

Critical Thinking Questions

1. Think of your favorite outdoor place to visit. What is one thing you could do to help take care of nature in that place?

2. Besides picking up litter and planting trees, what are some ways your family can care for nature?

3. Bees love flowers that smell good. They also love brightly colored flowers. Why should we care about bees? How do bees help nature?

Index